Copyright © Alliance of Independent Authors 2023, 2nd edition
First Edition, 2019.
The author's moral rights have been asserted.
All rights reserved.

Font Publications is the publishing imprint for Orna Ross's fiction and poetry, the Go Creative! books and planners, and the Alliance of Independent Authors publishing guides.

All Enquiries: info@ornaross.com

COPYRIGHT BILL OF RIGHTS
Eight Fundamental Rights for the Global Author in a Digital World
Ebook: 978-1-909888-92-0
Paperback: 978-1-909888-91-3

COPYRIGHT BILL OF RIGHTS

EIGHT FUNDAMENTAL RIGHTS FOR THE
GLOBAL AUTHOR IN A DIGITAL WORLD

ALLIANCE OF INDEPENDENT
AUTHORS

A book is the author's property, it is the child of his invention, the brat of his brain.

— DANIEL DEFOE.

'Tis the good reader that makes the good book.

— RALPH WALDO EMERSON.

CONTENTS

PART I
INTRODUCTION

Copyright and the Indie Author	3
Copyright and Author Income	9
Copyright Controversies	16

PART II
COPYRIGHT BILL OF RIGHTS

Right 1: The Right To Operate	31
Right 2: The Right To Link, License and Collaborate	33
Right 3: The Right to Fair Remuneration	35
Right 4: The Right to Fairness in Fair Dealing/Fair Use Frameworks	37
Right 5: The Right to Defend Copyright	40
Right 6: The Right to Coherence and Transparency	43
Right 7: The Right to Recognition in Machine Generated Works	45
Right 8: The Right to Copyright Education	48
The Future	51
Appendix I: A Short History of Copyright	56
Appendix II: Copyright FAQs	59
Appendix III: Business Models for Authors	67
Appendix IV: Copyright Organizations & Treaties	71
Acknowledgments	73
Other Guides	75
About ALLi	77

PART I
INTRODUCTION

COPYRIGHT AND THE INDIE AUTHOR

In the vast expanse that is today's literary world, independent authors have emerged as powerful voices, often pushing boundaries and reshaping the narrative landscape. 78% of authors responding to an ALLi survey on copyright in 2019 sell their work globally, in as many countries as possible. However, like all pioneers, they face unique challenges, and copyright is undeniably at the forefront.

The "Copyright Bill of Rights" campaign, initiated by the Alliance of Independent Authors, seeks to address these challenges head-on.

As the digital age accelerates and the world becomes increasingly interconnected, indie authors find themselves at the crossroads of creativity and commerce, striving to protect their creations while ensuring their works reach an ever-growing audience. Yet, the maze of copyright laws, originally designed in a bygone era, can hinder rather than help.

This campaign book from ALLi isn't just a guide; it's a manifesto. It champions the rights of indie authors, and offers tools and thoughts with which to navigate the intricate world of copyright today.

By outlining core principles to be upheld in the age of digital publishing and artificial intelligence, this campaign aspires to level the playing field, ensuring that indie authors are both protected and empowered. This isn't just about legalities; it's about fostering a culture that celebrates, supports, and sustains independent creativity.

How can we ensure that copyright law remains robust and flexible enough to offer the incentive, protection, and reward it promises for those authors who produce and distribute their books on self-publishing platforms, and license only some of their publishing rights to trade-publishers and other rights buyers? How can we ensure that authors understand and avail of their economic and moral rights in the rapidly changing, technologized, and entrepreneurial environment within which they do their work? And how do we achieve a balance between motivating creators through exclusive rights and upholding the public's interest by providing access to knowledge, information, and inspiration.

We present our answers to these important questions in the form of a *Bill of Rights* that builds on the work of previous authors and copyright activists to take into account the experience of self-publishing writers over the past decade, as digital publishing has increased in influenced.

About Copyright Law

The income that every author and publisher receives from the sale of books derives from copyright law. Independent authors, who are both writers and publishers, and who actively manage their own publishing rights, need to understand the importance of copyright, how to assert their rights in the digital age, and how those rights balance with the rights of others.

Copyright law is fundamental to an author's ability to publish and trade in books, create successful author-businesses, and to earn an income from their work.

Copyright has been recognized for centuries and is currently governed by the Copyright Act of 1976 in the US, the Copyright, Designs and Patents Act 1988 in the UK, and equivalent legislation in other countries. Copyright law protects "works of the mind," namely original work of literature, music, film, art, photography, sculpture, architecture, computer programs, databases, and more.

The law does not protect ideas, only their expression, or "fixation" as it is called in some jurisdictions. It recognizes that a creator owns the text, images, video, audio, information, and data created, and arising from that ownership, the creator has:

- the right to reproduce the work
- the right to prepare derivative works based upon the work
- the right to distribute copies of the work to the public
- the right to perform the copyrighted work publicly
- the right to display the copyrighted work publicly.

Copyright law gives authors the right to control the publication and other exploitation of the work. The author can decide whether to sell those rights, who to sell them to, and on what terms. Typically, rights are sold in the form of licenses, and the compensation is in the form of a flat fee or royalties.

Most of the problems and shortfalls for authors arise not in the law itself, but in its *execution*, with many rights buyers failing to observe it in letter or in spirit. Another problem is the polarization of authors' and readers' rights in copyright debates.

The law, publishing houses, and self-publishing services cannot offer authors full protection against plagiarism and piracy.

ALLi's *Copyright Bill of Rights* aims to inform and educate authors, industry practitioners, stakeholders, and policy-makers on the contemporary copyright environment for independent authors. It also offers ALLi's interpretation and recommendations of what authors and readers most need from copyright law, policy, and practice today.

The *Bill* is a work in progress, exploring with members, advisors, and like-minded authors' associations how copyright law, its related policies, and practical interpretations might provide better protection, incentive, and reward to authors who self-publish through online publishing platforms, as well as through licensing their publishing rights to other publishing entities.

The Independent Author

The independent author movement was born out of the digital technologies that emerged in the first decade of the twenty-first century. Authors have always self-published, but for the first time, technology provided authors the tools to inexpensively and directly attract and sell to a global readership, in ways that did not require an institutional publisher.

Using digital tools and technology, and supporting each other closely, independent authors currently conduct business in ways that render traditional discourse around rights and literary activity irrelevant.

ALLi members, located on all seven continents, represent the full spectrum of independent authorship, including literary and genre fiction and non-fiction, young adult and children's books, and poetry. All our members write *and* publish, or are preparing to publish, their own work.

Independent authors thus, being the creative directors of their books and also of their author enterprises, have the freedom and responsibility of full creative control. This is in contrast to those authors who are *creative professionals* following the traditional model of exclusively licensing publishing rights to a primary trade-publisher, usually with the help of a literary agent.

Independent authors work or collaborate with a team of professionals—other creatives like editors and designers, virtual assistants, agents, sub-agents, author services—to publish their own books and license their own rights. They are *creative entrepreneurs* (authorpreneurs), running highly scalable, nimble digital businesses that operate one of a number of possible business models (see Appendix III).

ALLi's **Authorpreneur Membership** category is for the most successful of these authors: author businesses that have sold more than 50,000 books, or the business equivalent, in the past two years. Such authors currently comprise almost 10 per cent of our membership.

Compared to authors who publish only through trade (traditional) publishing processes—who license their rights, are bound by exclusive, often needlessly circumscribed contracts, and have little or no control over their metadata or positioning in the marketplace—those who self-publish, or combine self-publishing and trade-publishing processes, are relatively autonomous. Hence "independent".

Without control over metadata, marketing, pricing, distribution network, or rights, an author is not actually in business. Another publisher has licensed their assets. The publisher has a business; the author is a freelance content provider for that business. With too many writers and too few publishers, the economic law of supply and demand creates poor conditions for authors.

If they have just one publisher, as most authors who trade-publish currently do, they are financially very vulnerable in a bookselling system built around a tiny minority of winners, and the vast pool of losers who don't attract an investing publisher, or who fail to sell in sufficient numbers to retain publisher investment.

The independent author, by contrast, can build a business step by step, asset by asset, over time.

To produce and sell their books and build and grow their author businesses, self-publishers hire help across some or all of the seven stages of the publishing process: editorial, design, production, distribution, marketing, promotion and rights licensing.

In pursuing their work, they encounter four kinds of publishing services:

1. **Self-publishing Companies Favorable to Authors:**
   Production and distribution services like Amazon KDP, Apple Books, Google Play (books), IngramSpark, Bookvault, Kobo Writing Life, aggregators like Draft2Digital, PublishDrive and StreetLib, along with freelance editorial, design, marketing and PR services (individuals or companies). ALLi provides a directory of recommended services to their members.
2. **Self-publishing Companies Exploitative of Authors:**
   Popularly known as "vanity publishers," these companies dominate the digital advertising space where they trap new

authors who are uninformed about how publishing and self-publishing works.
3. **Technology Companies:** Big tech platforms like Facebook, YouTube, Google Search, Bookbub and other tech platforms that enable author-publisher trading, social engagement, and book promotion.
4. **Content Companies aka Publishers:** Corporate or independent trade-publishers and media like Random House, Faber & Faber, News International, Hollywood that trade in author generated content.

The independent author depends on copyright law as incentive, reward and protection when dealing with these other players in the literary and publishing industries.

As you delve into these pages, you'll discover not only the foundations of a new copyright vision but also the collective aspirations of a vibrant community.

ALLi's Watchdog Desk regularly updates a directory of recommended self-publishing services. Members can download this directory for free by logging into the Members' Zone. Non-members can purchase a copy at: Selfpublishingadvice.org/directory/

COPYRIGHT AND AUTHOR INCOME

Author income is derived from the copyright applicable on the created work. Copyright law governs an author's ability to trade their rights on their own terms. All authors need to understand the basics of copyright law in order to protect their rights and maximize potential income.

In short, copyright gives authors the right to control not just the publication and sale of their books in their own language and territory but also the right to grant and license related rights to interested buyers. And the right to object to derogatory treatment, piracy or plagiarism of their unique expressions.

In the digital age, a piece of content can be uploaded in one country and downloaded in another within seconds. So what protections are afforded to the indie author who publishes to the world?

Copyright as Property

Countries that follow the Anglo-Saxon common law tradition, including the UK and the US, classify copyright as a property, which may be sold, assigned, licensed, bequeathed, or given away. In Europe, governed by a civil law tradition, *droit d'auteur* (the author's right) is a human, rather than property, right. European countries also place far more emphasis on the rights of the creator and on limiting the rights that may be transferred to others.

In practice, a copyright interest is treated as a piece of property, like your car or your home, but property of a special kind known as intellectual property. Other categories of intellectual property include patents, trademarks, and design rights. As the copyright holder, you have the right to control who uses your property. By law, these are the exclusive rights to:

- reproduce the work in books or other formats
- sell, distribute, and commercially exploit the work
- create derivative works, such as translations, adaptations, sequels, and abridgements, films, plays, or apps
- display or perform the work publicly, either live or in recorded form.

Without copyright law, anybody could reproduce, translate, adapt, or exploit any book without an obligation to acknowledge your interests, issue a license, or pay compensation.

Like your house or car, your copyright interest may be sold, assigned, licensed, given away, and bequeathed. When we talk about "selling" publishing rights what we're referring to is authors' legal right to grant permission (in the form of a license) to others to exploit some of their exclusive rights under the law—such as the right to reproduce the book in print or digital formats, or to translate the work, or to make a film based upon the work.

Each right may be licensed in exchange for compensation in the form of a flat fee or royalties (a percentage of sales revenue). ALLi's guide *How Authors Sell Publishing Rights* elucidates on selective rights licensing. This guide is available to purchase for non-members at Selfpublishingadvice.org/rights-licensing/. Members can download their free copy from the Members' Zone.

Unauthorized use of copyrighted work is almost always an infringement of rights and may entitle the copyright owner to obtain a court order to stop the infringing use and to recover monetary damages. In some cases, wilful infringement may subject the infringer to criminal charges.

Asserting Copyright

From an author's perspective, copyright is a passive right. An author who wants to engage it must assert ownership as a fact and, in cases of dispute, in a court of law. Copyright legislation has not prevented many self-publishing and trade-publishing companies from offering authors contracts that fail to align with the spirit, intention, or letter of the law.

ALLi's Watchdog desk regularly encounters unfair self-publishing and trade-publishing contracts that assign rather than license publishing rights, omit standard protection clauses, offer work-for-hire payment when royalties or commissions would be more ethical, and grab publishing rights which they have no plans to, or even intention of exploiting.

In addition to unfriendly contracts, piracy and plagiarism are flourishing in the digital age, with little consequence for those who infringe copyright. Piracy differs from plagiarism in that the pirate unlawfully distributes copies of an author's books, while the plagiarist repurposes another's work as their own.

> *They can also differ in legal standing. Copyright is about protecting the commercial rights of the author. Piracy is, at its core, an infringement on commercial rights. However, plagiarism is an ethical failure that may not fit the legal definition of copyright infringement. As a result, incidents of plagiarism may fail to meet the legal requirements of a copyright infringement suit — and often go unpunished.*
>
> — JOHN DOPPLER, HEAD OF ALLI'S WATCHDOG DESK

Both plagiarism and piracy can be unintentional or deliberate theft.

For example, a non-fiction writer might fail to properly credit a quoted passage or a person might download a free book without knowing it is copyright protected. Many publishing and self-publishing services have deliberately flouted, or circumvented, copyright law.

In the copyright debates, which we'll explore in more detail in the next chapter, author representative bodies have largely spoken as if author and publisher interests are aligned (they have little to say about self-publishing, either author-publishing or self-publishing services). Yet big content companies have not been fair to authors in their interpretation of copyright, as the same author organizations acknowledge in other aspects of their work for fairer contracts and more equitable treatment.

There has been some standardization of contracts among the largest and most reputable trade-publishers and self-publishing companies, but authors have traditionally suffered from a power imbalance in negotiations with publishers.

To the publishing and self-publishing industries, authors are content providers, creating the products upon which their profits are built. For authors, copyright assertion can sometimes be difficult and expensive to prove and may provide no protection anyway, as those who act illegally, by definition, have little respect for the law.

And even in cases of clear breach of law, few individual authors have the resources, or the will, to sue for copyright infringement.

The Misnomer of International Copyright

There is no international copyright.

Indie authors who distribute ebooks, audiobooks, and print-on-demand (POD) books globally would welcome consistent copyright laws protecting their content across territories and borders. Instead, international copyright law is based on a "combination of domestic legal systems, regional and international regimes, as well as bilateral and multilateral treaties and agreements."[1] These treaties, notably the "Berne Convention for the Protection of Literary and Artistic Works (Berne)"[2] and the Marrakesh Treaty[3], set out minimum copyright protections that must be extended by signatory nations. These treaties are administered by organizations like the World Intellectual Property Organization (WIPO). International trade agreements also play a role in international copyright law, but it is the copyright treaties that deal with specific copyright matters.

Domestic copyright legislation is based on the underlying philosophy prevalent in each country. Indie authors would benefit from an expanded understanding of how the philosophy of their own country's copyright law applies and differs from the laws of the jurisdictions in which they sell.

UK copyright law is underpinned by the philosophy of economics and the provision of monopolistic economic rights in an author's work.

EU copyright directives have standardized copyright law throughout the European Union, though each jurisdiction has separate and distinct laws and regulations.

For example, France offers the strongest moral rights, with a philosophy that aligns author rights with human rights, as opposed to a mere economic right. This *droit morale* protects an author's work as well as their reputation and extends to them the right to decide how and whether to be identified as the author of the work.

The US uses economic theory as the basis for its copyright law, resulting in fairly strong rights for authors and copyright owners. These rights are juxtaposed against a long list of exceptions for users. Moral rights in the US do not extend to authors.

In Canada, copyright law is based on a combined European/UK philosophy, protecting economic rights to authors and copyright owners as well as provisions around moral rights.

Despite these differences, minimum requirements for copyright protection established by Berne have been adopted by nearly 200 signatory countries.

NATIONAL TREATMENT

Berne's underlying principle is national treatment: where the work is *used* determines the law that applies.

As an author, your copyright interest is largely subject to the law in the country where you reside and will be recognized in most countries. However, the concept of "national treatment" means that if someone in another country wishes to access, copy, or re-use portions of your work, for example photocopying an article, the copyright law in the country where the action occurs is applied. Each country has its own terms of protection.

Automatic Protection

Berne requires member countries to extend copyright protection automatically, as soon as the idea is "fixed," that is written down or recorded.

A work does not need to be registered for copyright to take effect, though registration can provide proof in the event of a dispute and in some jurisdictions, notably the US, where copyright registration has been used in law courts as proof of ownership. In fact, the US didn't sign on to Berne until 1989, as prior to that time copyright protection was not automatic and first required registration.

Duration of Protection

Berne requires copyright protection, and its right to control publishing, copying, and other exploitations of the works, for a minimum of fifty years after an author's death (life-plus-fifty), after which it becomes public domain. In the US, EU, and UK, the duration is life-plus-seventy.

The globalization of commerce and the exponential growth of the digital age have posed new challenges and considerations for copyright law across nations. As commerce becomes increasingly global, there's pressure for countries to harmonize their copyright laws, leading to debates about the best approach and concerns about larger, more powerful nations dictating terms.

There's no one-size-fits-all in copyright law. What works for one country, given its cultural, economic, and social context, might not work for another. The question then arises: Should countries adopt a minimum standards approach, where basic tenets are agreed upon, or should they strive for fuller harmonization?

While the harmonization of copyright laws in an increasingly globalized world seems logical, the path to achieving it is fraught with challenges. It requires a delicate balance between international cooperation and respect for individual national contexts.

Larger, economically powerful countries might exert disproportionate influence in shaping international copyright standards, potentially prioritizing their own interests over those of smaller nations. Rigidly harmonized copyright laws might force countries to make changes to their existing laws, leading to concerns about loss of sovereignty and the ability to make decisions that best serve their citizens.

Major multinational corporations, with vast resources and global reach, might lobby for copyright harmonization that benefits their business models, possibly at the expense of smaller entities and individual creators.

The evolution of copyright law and the controversies surrounding it are deeply intertwined with societal, technological, and economic changes. Let's take a closer look at some of those controversies.

---

1. Practical International Copyright, Copyright Laws.com. April 2018. https://www.copyrightlaws.com
2. *Berne Convention for the Protection of Literary Works*, 1886, last amended 1979. https://www.wipo.int/treaties/en/text.jsp?file_id=283698#P140_25350
3. WIPO. *Marrakesh Treaty to Facilitate Access to Published Works for Persons Who Are Blind, Visually Impaired, or Otherwise Print Disabled.* https://www.wipo.int/treaties/en/ip/marrakesh/

COPYRIGHT CONTROVERSIES

Copyright is a complex area of law, and as with many areas of law, it can give rise to a range of controversies. As we have seen, copyright aims to strike a balance between incentivizing creators by granting them exclusive rights and serving the public interest by allowing access to creative works. Achieving and holding this balance is inherently contentious.

Innovations, especially in digital technology, have radically altered how content is produced, distributed, and consumed. The internet, for instance, made copying and sharing content effortless, leading to conflicts between traditional copyright frameworks and new modes of consumption.

Unlike tangible property, intellectual property is non-rivalrous. This means multiple people can consume an intellectual good (like a song or book) without it being "used up". This unique characteristic makes defining and enforcing property rights challenging.

There's debate over the economic impact of copyright, with some arguing that strict copyright protections stifle innovation and others contending that they're essential for incentivizing creativity. In the realm of academic publishing, debates arise around the ethics of limiting access to (sometimes life-saving) knowledge through copyright and patent protections.

Copyright protection doesn't last indefinitely. However, the length of time that works remain copyrighted has been extended several times, especially in the U.S., often in response to lobbying by major corporations. Critics argue these extensions prevent works from entering the public domain in a timely manner and that they benefit large corporations more than individual creators.

The doctrine of fair use allows for the unlicensed use of copyrighted material in certain circumstances, such as criticism, comment, news reporting, teaching, scholarship, and research. However, the boundaries of fair use are not always clear, leading to debates and lawsuits about what constitutes fair use.

DRM (Digital Rights Management) technologies attempt to control the use, modification, and distribution of copyrighted works. Critics (including ALLi) argue that DRM restricts users' rights to access and modify legally-acquired content and can make it difficult for people to exercise their fair use rights. It can really irritate readers.

Some entities purchase copyrights or obtain the rights to enforce copyrights not to produce or distribute the content, but to threaten alleged infringers with lawsuits and seek settlements. This has led to concerns about the misuse of the legal system for profit.

That copyright has real and significant value can be seen in how it is ever more vehemently contested by three competing interests regularly contesting each other across the digital battleground:

- **Big Tech:** Internet publishing platforms like Google, Facebook and Amazon that authors use to publish and/or promote books on.
- **Big Content:** global media corporations like Penguin Random House, News International and Hollywood to whom authors license publishing rights. Here we also find large self-publishing services like Author Solutions, some of whom grab rights as well as charge service fees.

- **Big Legal:** Large legislating territories and blocks like the European Union who aim to modify the power of big tech and big content.

All of these affect how self-publishers work and earn but none speak directly to, or for, independent authors. Neither do trade-publishers, literary agents nor, sadly, many authors' organizations.

The interests of an Internet tech giant like Google or Facebook; a social media company like X or LinkedIn, a news organization like The Guardian or New York Times, a traditional publishing house like Random House or Penguin, a literary agency, a legislative body, a trade-published author, or even an authors' representative body, may not align with those of the independent, self-publishing author.

Independent authors know from experience that Big Tech companies are not all equal in their treatment of copyright. There is a vast difference between how Amazon, Kobo or IngramSpark, one one hand, treat authors and other creators when compared to, for example, YouTube or Meta.

Credit is due to publishing tech platforms who have respected copyright in their business models. Amazon's innovative KDP platform, with its combination of ebooks, Kindle ereader and online bookstore, has allowed countless authors to earn significant income, and enjoy significant impact and influence through self-publishing. It has inspired other innovative and effective publishing tech in text, voice, and video.

All of this is benefitting independent authors, allowing them to set up successful and sustainable author businesses. As author confidence grows, we see more writers setting up businesses that incorporate a variety of tech platforms, centered around their own websites and employing a variety of business models. See ALLi's **SelfPub3 Campaign** at Allianceindependentauthors.org/selfpub3/ for more on author businesses.

Copyright Curtail and Control

The experiences of self-publishing authors need to be considered and weighed in copyright debate and policy, particularly by those who purport to speak on authors' behalf.

The copyright industry's ability to curtail and control has been blown apart by digital and AI technology—the explosion in author, personal, and organizational publishing; the Internet's free copying and remix culture; the magnitude and global reach of peer-to-peer file sharing, illegal downloads, plagiarism and piracy.

Contrary to the claims of Big Content (and the author representative bodies that unfortunately support their assertions), new technologies have not been detrimental to authors in the main. They have democratized the publishing process, empowered authors to engage directly with their readers, enabled authors to monetize their skills in new ways and unleashed a ferment of creativity.

Our copyright deliberations to date have revealed that many interested parties, including some authors and author associations, do not understand the self-publishing trading environment or, indeed, how books are traded today. In consequence, there is a danger that ideas and campaigns around copyright that purport to speak for authors' rights might actually be detrimental to the author who operates independently.

Misinformation about Self-Publishing

A great deal of misinformation about self-publishing circulates in the literary, publishing, and creative industries, and the associated trade and government bodies that engage with them. And there's a lot of lip service by Big Content companies who regularly use author rights protection when fighting what is actually a business dispute between them and Big Tech.

"Authors are always at the forefront of copyright debates... whether it's arguments in favor of broader and longer rights, or against new uses for

> *the broader public... But if you're an author yourself, you might have noticed something puzzling... that, for someone who plays such a prominent role in the debate, surprisingly little of the rewards actually trickle down to you."*
>
> — ASSOCIATE PROFESSOR REBECCA GIBLIN, THE AUTHOR'S INTEREST

On many issues around remuneration, independent authors have more in common with creative entrepreneurs in other sectors like music, art, tech, and education than with authors who publish exclusively through the traditional agent-publisher-wholesaler-bookstore supply chain.

Who Should Benefit?

The very concept of copyright has been hotly contested, based on what Kevin Kelly of *Wired* magazine has called a profound riddle: *Who should benefit most from works of the mind, the creators or society at large?*

On the one side are those who argue strongly that creators must be paid for their work and see copyright as the best mechanism to ensure that they are. On the other are those who believe that, by granting an author (or a large corporation such as Disney) exclusive rights to a work for decades, the law is limiting the free flow of information, education, and inspiration. This tension has deepened, as the markets for literary work expand, and technology raises new questions.

Traditionally copyright's tug of interest has been a *pas de trois* between author, publisher, and reader. For the independent author, it's a *pas de deux*, a balancing of author rights and reader rights.

Authors want copyright to deliver the rewards everyone wants from hard work: appropriate remuneration and recognition. The reader, whose interest is also protected by copyright, wants easy and reasonably priced access to good content.

Current conflicts between these two interests pit creators, content companies, Hollywood and governments on one side against readers, pirates, Silicon Valley, and open-access advocates on the other.

The copyright industries, with the support of some powerful authors' organizations, argue, in the words of the UK Society of Authors (SoA), that:

> ...sharing illegal copies for free online means publishers lose out on sales and authors lose out on royalties. It also leads to a decline in the perceived value of a book.
>
> — UK SOCIETY OF AUTHORS "WHERE WE STAND"

For these copyright activists, file sharing is theft. As SoA Chair and world-renowned trade-published author, Philip Pullman, put it: "... *as surely as reaching into someone's pocket and taking their wallet is theft.*"

On the opposite side to the authors' interest organizations is the "copy left", or "free culture movement". This diverse group of activists, artists, lawyers, and scholars, which includes movements like open source software and Creative Commons licensing, challenge traditional copyright models by promoting more permissive licensing and the idea that some content should be freely sharable and modifiable.

They urge authors and other creators towards a keener understanding of how to best exploit their own publishing rights in the digital age, rather than trying to curtail others. They question the wisdom of trying to impose a twentieth-century exclusive-rights copyright regime on the digital landscape of the twenty-first century.

They fear excessive legal restrictions will endanger many invaluable knowledge and entertainment initiatives, from crowdsourced, "read-write websites" like Wikipedia to authors writing within another author's fictional world.

And they oppose attempts to cordon off copyrighted material (digital rights management) as ineffective and ideologically unsound. Instead, they argue for the individual author's right to set their own rights terms in Creative Commons agreements and quote evidence indicating that piracy, counter-intuitively, does not actually have a derogatory effect on author income.

One such copyleft activist is our own Dan Holloway, ALLi's news editor. In a blog post on the Self Publishing Advice Center "Indie Authors Need to Talk About Copyright", he says: "I'm a firm believer in open access in the very widest sense – making "the whole sum of human knowledge available to everyone with an internet connection". Like others who think on similar lines, I take this position because I believe creativity matters, not because I believe it doesn't. I believe it matters so much that the freedom to be creative cannot be allowed to rely on something so fragile as the protection afforded by copyright.

"Because copyright is, fundamentally, a means to ensure payment. So to place copyright on a pedestal is to make the freedom to be creative, depend on the ability to secure payment for the product (word used advisedly) of that creativity."

Between these two polarized positions sits the independent author, relying on both copyright law and large internet firms for their living.

The experience of the self-publishing author introduces much needed nuance into the debate and shows clearly that pitting author against "user" is an oversimplification that ignores how we buy, borrow, read, and write books in the digital age.

Authors are not simply creators in need of recompense and protection. We are also readers, researchers, scholars, and citizens seeking education, imaginative stimulation and inspiration. Digital publishing has moved us from a scarcity model around books to an abundance model. If we fail to recognize that, we are in danger of hurting more authors than we help.

For example, under current law, scanning a copyrighted work and making it available for display on the internet without permission is an infringement. Then along came the Google mass digitization project: Google Book Search, with the aspiration to make all of the world's printed books available for digital search, without charge, for anyone with access to the internet.

Should the law be different if, instead of one book, it's twenty million? The US courts think so.

A US District Court determined that Google's mass digitization of copyrighted works, making the works searchable and readable in "snippets," qualified as an exception under fair use. The ruling was affirmed on appeal, and the case was then heard by the US Supreme Court which also sided with Google.

The US Authors Guild led this legal battle against Google's project.

The digital revolution cannot come at the cost of authors' rights to preserve writing as a livelihood.

— US AUTHORS GUILD

Yet many independent authors see the Google Book Search project as benefitting, not hurting their author-businesses. They want to be easily searchable and findable online. They know the biggest problem today's author faces is obscurity, and welcome any tool that help readers find their way to their book.

They want potential readers to be able to identify their books as being germane to their search inquiry. They want Google to locate the pages on which the search term appears for the reader, and to give a sense of what their book has to say about the search term.

For the reader—and nobody reads more than authors—Google's Book Search project gives what Neil Winstock Netanel describes as:

...ready access to a global, virtual library card catalog, with the huge added value of being able to apply search engine queries to the entire text of every book, view the full text of public domain materials, and receive information about where to locate or buy copyright-protected materials.

— NEIL WINSTOCK NETANEL, COPYRIGHT'S PARADOX

Copyright laws or vested "authors' interest" lobbies that fail to acknowledge that we have moved from a scarcity to an abundance economy for books, and that fail to preserve and strengthen the symbiosis of the writer-reader relationship, fail writers as well as readers.

Freebies and The Gift Economy

A book is not a commodity like the proverbial can of beans. It is freely produced through the gifts and talents of the author and gains in value from the act of being circulated—published, shown, written about, passed on. At its core, it is an offering: a gift.

In his fascinating book, *The Gift*, Lewis Hyde cites Homer's Hymn to Hermes, saying:

To bestow one of our creations is the surest way to invoke the next. Hermes invents the first musical instrument, the lyre, and gives it to his brother, Apollo, whereupon he is immediately inspired to invent a second musical instrument, the pipes. The implication is that giving the first creation away makes the second one possible.

Bestowal creates that empty place into which new energy may flow. The alternative is petrification, writer's block, 'the flow of life backed up'.

— LEWIS HYDE. *THE GIFT: HOW THE CREATIVE SPIRIT TRANSFORMS THE WORLD*

Authors are much closer than trade-publishers to this understanding, and many agree with Walt Whitman that "the gift is to the giver, and comes back most to him – it cannot fail" and are happy to freely circulate some, or even all, of their books.

At a more business-like level, other authors use a freemium model, a pricing strategy that offers some part of a product or service free but then charges for additional features, services, or goods.

Many authors are using freemium to great effect, with having a free first book in series being a very common strategy used by successful indie authors, or using free books to attract readers to courses or other more highly-priced associated material.

AI and Copyright

The intersection of artificial intelligence and augmented intelligence (AI) and copyright is spurring a whole new category of controversies and debates. As AI systems become more sophisticated and create content that once required human intervention, the traditional frameworks of copyright are being challenged.

Here are the key points of contention:

- **Ownership of AI-Generated Content**: One of the central questions is: Who owns the rights to content generated by AI? Is it the developer of the AI system, the user who utilized the AI, or does no one own it since a human didn't directly create it? Current copyright frameworks in many jurisdictions are built around human authorship, so AI-generated content presents a conundrum.
- **Originality and Creativity**: Copyright protection is often granted to works that exhibit originality or creativity. If an AI is trained on existing copyrighted content and produces something new based on that training, is the result truly original? Or is it merely a derivative of the data it was fed?
- **Economic Implications**: If AI-generated content is not copyrightable, it might flood the market with freely available material. This could devalue human-created content or alter business models across industries, from music and art to journalism and software development.
- **Moral Rights**: In some jurisdictions, beyond economic rights, copyright encompasses moral rights. These are rights of the creator to be acknowledged as the author of a work and to object to derogatory treatments of their works. With AI-generated content, the application of moral rights becomes complex.

- **Liability for Infringement**: If an AI inadvertently creates content that infringes on existing copyrights, who is liable? The developer? The user? Or is no one liable due to the lack of human intent?
- **Training Data Concerns**: AI systems, particularly machine learning models, require vast amounts of data for training. If copyrighted material is used in this training process without authorization, does it constitute infringement?
- **Using AI as a Co-creator**: In scenarios where AI aids human creators (e.g., suggesting music chords or writing assists), determining where the AI's contribution ends and the human's begins can be murky. Who then should be credited or bear the responsibility for the final product?
- **Future of Human Creativity**: Philosophically, there's a debate over the role of AI in creative processes. Does heavy reliance on AI tools diminish the value of human creativity? Or does it merely represent another tool, like a camera or a paintbrush, in the hands of creators?
- **International Harmonization**: Different countries might adopt varied approaches to AI and copyright. This could lead to challenges in enforcing and recognizing copyrights on AI-generated content internationally.

As AI continues to evolve and becomes more integrated into creative and professional domains, these controversies are intensifying. The legal community, policymakers, AI developers, and content creators are engaging in collaborative discussions and legal court cases which are reshaping the future of copyright in the age of AI.

The Alliance of Independent Authors policy in relation to AI can be found here: Selfpublishingadvice.org/ai

Copyright Is Now Mainstream

The digital revolution has made copyright and its violation a news story that extends far beyond authors. Blogging, podcasting, video creation and social media allows everyone to be a self-publisher, moving copyright issues into the mainstream.

Early in 2019, opposition to a proposed EU Copyright Directive (now passed) saw, among other protests, an online petition[1] gather more than five million signatures, a Polish newspaper printing a blank front page[2], Italian Wikipedia blacking out, and concerned German citizens[3] taking to the streets. Many of the protesters against Article 13 (now Article 17) of the controversial EU Directive were authors and other creators. They did not want the changes Big Content (third-party publishers) were asking for, purportedly on their behalf.

These authors want the free and flexible internet we already have and believe that the foundational copyright law we have is already robust and flexible enough to meet today's needs. They are concerned that some changes which Big Content depicts as updating and improving copyright law for the digital age does not work well for independent authors and their readers.

Within the self-publishing community itself, indie authors take many different approaches and hold widely varying opinions about copyright issues like piracy, plagiarism and digital rights management, from those who are copyright vigilant to those who welcome piracy as a form of marketing.

The experience of the self-publishing author introduces much needed nuance into the debate and shows clearly that pitting author against "user" is an oversimplification that ignores how we buy, borrow, read, and write books in the digital age.

Authors are not simply creators in need of recompense and protection. We are also readers, researchers, scholars, and citizens seeking education, imaginative stimulation and inspiration.

Digital publishing has moved us from a scarcity model around books to an abundance model. Generative AI moves us into a world where words are easily produced than ever before.

The biggest danger to authors today is not copying but obscurity. You can write a great book, but in the midst of all the great work out there, how is your reader going to find you?

Within the self-publishing community itself, indie authors take many different approaches and hold widely varying opinions about copyright issues like piracy, plagiarism, and digital rights management. But copyright laws or vested "authors' interest" lobbies that fail to acknowledge the impact of AI, the abundance economy for books, and the need for copyright to protect readers' rights, fail writers too.

Legislation that focusses heavily on authors' rights, without an understanding of the symbiotic relationship between author and reader, without a realistic assessment of how books and their associated products are discovered, purchased, read, and marketed today, without an understanding of how most entrepreneurial creators work, trade, and negotiate harms more authors and readers than it helps.

A healthy, supportive, and functioning global copyright environment balances the benefits of ownership with the flexibility we need to run a successful and sustainable business.

---

1. Change.org. *Stop the censorship machinery! Save the Internet!* https://www.change.org/p/european-parliament-stop-the-censorship-machinery-save-the-internet
2. France24. *Polish dailies print blank front page in EU copyright appeal.* March 25, 2019. https://www.france24.com/en/20190325-polish-dailies-print-blank-front-page-eu-copyright-appeal
3. CNBC. *Thousands protest against controversial EU internet law claiming it will enable online censorship.* March 25, 2019. https://www.cnbc.com/2019/03/25/protesters-in-germany-say-new-eu-law-will-enable-online-censorship.html

PART II

COPYRIGHT BILL OF RIGHTS

RIGHT 1: THE RIGHT TO OPERATE

Authors have the right to operate as publishers and creative entrepreneurs, within a copyright system that facilitates author credit and compensation but does not suppress free speech or expression.

Independent authors' right to operate rests on a legal copyright framework which facilitates:

- authors and authorpreneurs to trade in books and other intellectual property in a digital publishing environment
- self-investment with appropriate returns
- sharing and distribution of content in text, audio and video for promotion purposes.

The right to promote and to link inwards and out is integral to the right to operate online author business.

Self-publishing authors are accustomed to signing licensing agreements with book hosting and trading platforms like Amazon, Apple Books, Kobo, Google Books and IngramSpark.

Such online services employ filtering systems to reduce

unauthorized reproductions of copyright-protected works, and as part of their monetization programs to compensate copyright owners.

For copyright purposes, these systems are built on top of a database containing lists of individual copyrighted works and their owners. The system scans all material uploaded to identify any part of an upload that matches an entry in the database.

These systems cannot decide whether the use of content is actually unauthorized or might be acceptable under a limitation or exception to copyright, such as fair use/dealing (See Right 4). Author-publishers already know from experience that upload filters and algorithms are error-prone, and cannot differentiate between copyright infringements and legal use.

Upon finding a match, the system may either block access to the upload, take steps to associate it with a monetization program, or take some other action such as notifying the copyright owner or asking for proof of copyright ownership.

Under the recent EU Copyright Directive, platforms like Facebook, Pinterest, and YouTube who had resisted recompensing copyright holders will now be required to install similar filters. This law is a fundamental change to copyright and publishing on the internet.

This legislation is likely to add to independent author burden as the onus is now on the copyright holder to prove ownership against the "decisions" of the filter.

A small proportion of high-earning, high-traffic authors whose websites and worlds attract uploads from other authors and creators may fall also within the remit of the Directive. At the moment platforms or services with under €10 million in revenue, or which have existed for less than three years, or with fewer than five million monthly users, are exempted.

Article One: *Copyright law, policy, and practice must facilitate authors' right to operate business, by enabling appropriate incentives, rewards and protections for self-publishers and recognition of how books are bought, sold and promoted in a digital environment.*

RIGHT 2: THE RIGHT TO LINK, LICENSE AND COLLABORATE

Authors have a right to grant sharing permission to other content creators as they see fit. The contemporary impulse to think of culture as "intellectual property" contains far more "property" than the original activists who won copyright for authors intended.

Redressing the balance between private (corporate, individual) and common (public) interests depends not just on effective policy but also on recovering the idea of the cultural commons.

"All Rights Reserved" is the copyright default but a considerable portion of authors want to share their work under other terms. Creative Commons is a licensing system that allows the creator to link out, license, and collaborate more freely.

Copyright is a passive right that comes into play as soon as words are written. Creative Commons adds an active dimension, where the author specifies the precise level of control they want to maintain over their work.

Creative Commons licenses exchange control in relation to other content creators for more control in relation to publishing platforms. By granting explicit sharing permissions to other content creators, the ability of hosting platforms to appropriate rights is limited.

Many authors are also exploring new revenue-sharing options, e.g. voluntary blanket licenses or pooled copyrights as well as royalties and commissions. New technology like the blockchain will facilitate such creator-led payment chains, by facilitating payment splits at the point of transaction.

Article Two: *Copyright law, policy, and practice must facilitate authors' rights to set the terms on which their work may be read, shared or distributed.*

RIGHT 3: THE RIGHT TO FAIR REMUNERATION

Independent authors have the right to fair remuneration from publishing and self-publishing companies who trade in their copyright. Fair remuneration is affected by other parts of the copyright ecosystem, including fair contracts, rights licensing, and fair use/fair dealing (see Right 4).

In order to be fairly remunerated, data provided by self-publishing platforms and trade-publishers must be accurately reported and revenue splits must be equitable.

Fair remuneration is also about the ability to build an author business and receive support that enables them to meet the challenges inherent in being both creator and publisher, particularly in the early stages of becoming an effective author-publisher and building an author business.

There has been some standardization of contracts among the largest and most reputable trade-publishers and self-publishing companies but most authors are ignorant of the incentive, reward, and protection clauses that should be in a publishing or self-publishing contract and have traditionally suffered from a power imbalance in any negotiation.

> *Authors can suffer from significant inequality of bargaining power and asymmetry of information in their dealings with cultural investors (such as publishers). That can mean they end up transferring all or most of their rights as condition of distribution or investment. What authors transfer can be disproportionate to what they get in return.*
>
> — ASSOCIATE PROFESSOR REBECCA GIBLIN, MONASH UNIVERSITY, AUSTRALIA AND THE AUTHOR'S INTEREST WEBSITE.

In negotiations with trade-publishers and other rights buyers, self-publishing authors who have built a following should be entitled to higher revenue splits than a beginning author with only the rights in a manuscript to trade.

Authors themselves need to value their moral and economic rights and be prepared to defend them as they enter negotiations with rights buyers and self-publishing services.

Article Three: *Copyright law, policy, and practice must facilitate authors' right to a fair share of the income generated by their work.*

RIGHT 4: THE RIGHT TO FAIRNESS IN FAIR DEALING/FAIR USE FRAMEWORKS

Authors have the right to participate in a fair dealing/fair use framework that equitably balances the economic rights of copyright holders with the moral rights of readers.

Fair use (US, Israel, Philippines) and fair dealing (Commonwealth countries like Canada, the UK, Australia) are similar, providing exceptions to copyright. These exception provisions are *user centered* (a user's right to access copyrighted material), *not creator centered* (the author's right to restrict sharing and distribution of their copyrighted work in cases deemed to support the public good).

There is no fair use/dealing clauses in EU legislation. This, combined with Articles 17 (formerly 13) and 11 of the recent EU Directive is of great concern to all who care about reader and user rights. Authors rely on these rights to create their own works.

Fair use/dealing limits the instances in which copyright owners can require payment, with significant and positive effect for educators, students, creative professionals, and entrepreneurs like authors, journalists and filmmakers, and individuals who, in their daily lives, wish to use, copy, or share portions of copyright protected works. It presumes that use is of an extent to not affect the copyright holder's exclusive rights[1] to reproduce or otherwise use the work.

Use of copyright material that goes beyond the scope of fair use/dealing is "unauthorized use" and a violation of copyright law. For independent and other authors, the result is real economic harm.

Fair use/dealing clauses give the courts four factors to consider when determining whether a particular use of a work is "fair":

- the purpose and character of the use;
- the nature of the copyrighted work;
- the amount and substantiality of the portion used in relation to the work as a whole;
- and the effect of the use on the potential market for, or value of, the original work.

No single factor determines the outcome; it's about balance. One or more may cancel out or accentuate another.

Evaluating fair use/dealing therefore requires a comprehensive knowledge of the original work and its potential markets; an awareness of the context in which the new use appears; and the ability to recognize complex concepts like parody or today's internet and remix culture.

Judging fair use/dealing is rarely a straightforward process. It may be possible to automate it in the future, but it currently depends on human review.

Before the EU Copyright Directive, Section 512 of the Digital Millennium Copyright Act (US)[2] and Article 14 of the E-Commerce Directive (EU)[3] allowed service providers to avoid liability for any infringing acts of their users as long as they removed the allegedly infringing content after notification.

But—and this is crucial—users also had the opportunity to challenge removals if they believe their post to have been non-infringing.

Upload filters, however, leave users with no recourse for posts blocked by the filter. This is the aspect of the EU Directive that drew protest from so many[4]. In the wake of the EU Copyright Directive, the reading, writing, teaching, and research world must now rely on private companies to ensure that EU copyright policies do not restrict reader freedoms worldwide.

Article Four: *Copyright law, policy, and practice must facilitate authors' and readers' rights to fair use/dealing.*

---

1. US Copyright Office Fair Use Index. https://www.copyright.gov/fair-use/more-info.html
2. Cornell Law School, Legal Information Institute. *U.S. Code, Title 17, Copyrights Chapter 5, Copyright Infringement and Remedies, Section 512: Limitations on liability relating to material online.* https://www.law.cornell.edu/uscode/text/17/512 Accessed May 12, 2019.
3. EU E-Commerce Directive. *Directive 2000/31/EC of the European Parliament and of the Council of 8 June 2000 on certain legal aspects of information society services, in particular electronic commerce, in the Internal Market ('Directive on electronic commerce')* . https://eur-lex.europa.eu/LexUriServ/LexUriServ.do?uri=CELEX:32000L0031:en:HTML
4. #SaveYourInternet. *Raise Your Voice and Act Against Article 17 [ex Art. 13].* https://saveyourinternet.eu/act/

RIGHT 5: THE RIGHT TO DEFEND COPYRIGHT

Authors have the right to be free from theft and to have adequate copyright protection tools, safeguards, and penalties in place for those who deliberately plagiarize, pirate, or otherwise unlawfully use their work, to the detriment of their economic rights.

This also includes the right to fair contracts with trade-publishers, with protection for authors pressured to sign unfair, unclear, or outdated contacts.

Book piracy robs many authors of their economic rights. The UK Intellectual Property Office estimates 17 percent of ebooks are consumed illegally[1]. The Guardian newspaper surveyed readers about book piracy[2] and found ebook pirates are mainly between age thirty and sixty, and come from the better-off socioeconomic groups. The majority of the readers saw nothing wrong in the practice.

Twenty-five percent of Canadian respondents cited in a 2017 report[3] into online copyright infringement had consumed at least one illegally-obtained file in the preceding three months. Almost half of them reported being unsure of what is legal. And, indeed, the legal and tech aspects of book piracy prevention are complex and fast-evolving.

Some ALLi members frequently ask for help removing their copyrighted works from pirate sites. Others are happy to be pirated, believing—like those who chose to give away free books—that piracy is a less significant problem for authors than obscurity. Some even use piracy as a marketing tool.

It's also worth noting that although there are hundreds of sites claiming to have pirated works, many are actually credit card scams, malware distributors, or other criminal operations using scraped listings from Amazon and other sources as bait to lure victims.

Systems that ensure copyright owners can notify online service providers of infringement are available in both the US[4] and the EU for now[5]. When a copyright owner discovers that a web-hosting company is housing unlawful material, a DMCA notice in writing to the web-hosting company is the method used to demand takedown.

Although technically a US law, the existence of the Digital Millennium Copyright Act (1998) allows similar action to be taken in all territories[6]. However, individual DMCA takedown notices are largely ineffective.

ALLi's Watchdog desk describes it as "whack-a-mole". For example, one of the most persistent ebook pirate sites, with over 120,000 take-down notices against it, has been taken down multiple times, only to emerge again under a different .com, .net, or .org domain name. Threats from lawyers, domain hosts, and the police have done nothing to stop it.

Governments, working together with search engines and internet service providers, could establish an enforcement arm — or fund such a body within existing law enforcement agencies — to help investigate, police, and shut down the most blatant thefts and exploitations.

Article Five: *Copyright law, policy, and practice should include safeguards to make copyright defensible.*

---

1. UK Intellectual Property Office, *Online Copyright Infringement Tracker (7th Wave)* March 2017. https://www.gov.uk/government/publications/online-copyright-infringement-tracker-survey-7th-wave

2. Guest, Katy, *'I Can Get Any Novel I Want in 30 Seconds': Can Book Piracy be Stopped?* London, UK: The Guardian, March 6, 2019 https://www.theguardian.com/books/2019/mar/06/i-can-get-any-novel-i-want-in-30-seconds-can-book-piracy-be-stopped
3. Innovation, Science, and Economic Development Canada. *Study of Online Consumption of Copyrighted Content: Attitudes Toward and Prevalence of Copyright Infringement in Canada – Final Report.* July 2017. https://www.ic.gc.ca/eic/site/112.nsf/eng/07648.html#a04
4. Cornell Law School, Legal Information Institute. *U.S. Code, Title 17, Copyrights Chapter 5, Copyright Infringement and Remedies, Section 512: Limitations on liability relating to material online.* https://www.law.cornell.edu/uscode/text/17/512 Accessed May 12, 2019.
5. DMCA. *Description of the DMCA Takedown Process in the European Union,* Modified: 09/16/2018. https://www.dmca.com/faq/European-DMCA-Takedown-process
6. DMCA. *Description of the DMCA Takedown Process in the European Union.*

RIGHT 6: THE RIGHT TO COHERENCE AND TRANSPARENCY

The current technical and legal infrastructure around copyright is often incoherent and fails to establish whether IP has the status of personal property, e.g. goods or land; the extent to which the rules governing IP are different from or the same as the rules governing other types of property; and the particular reach and remit of copyright law (as contract and commercial as well as intellectual property law).

There is also, in most jurisdictions, a failure to consider or properly clarify the different requirements of different kinds of IP (e.g. copyright versus patents) and related legal issues, including inconsistency of treatment across different countries, even in issues as central and crucial as fair use/dealing.

Dealings around the EU Directive were so confusing that a number of MEPs (Members of European Parliament) accidentally voted the wrong way on amendments.

In implementation, coherence and transparency are also important. Publishing contracts are notoriously difficult to interpret and incoherence around the value of copyright has allowed Big Tech companies like Facebook to profit greatly from their users' personal data without any recompense.

Article Six: *Copyright law, policy, and practice should be coherent and transparent, taking into account the global trade of self-publishing authors and digital platforms.*

RIGHT 7: THE RIGHT TO RECOGNITION IN MACHINE GENERATED WORKS

Traditionally, copyright in computer-generated works was not in question. The *program* was a tool that supported the creative process, just like pen and paper. But with the latest types of artificial intelligence, the computer program is no longer a tool; it actually makes many of the decisions involved in the creative process without human intervention.

The word "human" does not appear at all in copyright law, leaving AI's place in copyright unclear.

Copyright law does not yet clearly define who "owns" machine-generated works, or the role played by the humans in creation of the work. Depending on how law is made, there is a danger that AI systems will become not just a valuable tool assisting and inspiring creativity but another way to exploit and underpay writers, musicians, and artists.

Can an AI "system" claim legal authorship of the text it produces? Behind every such system are the humans who created the software. Are they the authors?

The answers to many of these questions are unclear. The Compendium of US Copyright Office Practices[1], an internal staff guidebook for the Copyright Office, does outline that humanness is a requirement for being an author, under the law. It's called "The Human Authorship Requirement," and it means plants or animals can't be authors. Neither can supernatural beings or "works produced by a machine or mere mechanical process that operates randomly or automatically without any creative input or intervention from a human author." It says nothing, as yet, on AI.

Another question arises with AI in relation to copyright. Can AI legally be trained on copyrighted text?

Until law is established, ALLi recommends that all machine generated works should be governed by agreements, in writing, that clarify ownership, with all contributors identified, tracked, and compensated.

Blockchain technology may help here. ALLi collaborator Access Copyright (and Prescient Innovations, the creator-focused innovation lab it founded) has proposed a framework they call "the three As" of trackable, auditable content: attribution, authentication, and automation.

1. **Attribution**: content makes clear who the creators and rights holders are, even as it moves around.
2. **Authentication**: content is clear on who does and who does not have access rights.
3. **Automation**: content is governed by defined rules that allow automatic transactions and splits at point of sale.

The aim is to offer an irrefutable link between the work and its copyright holder in a way that is authoritative, public, transparent, and auditable.

Article Seven: Copyright law, policy, and practice should enable the right to author attribution in machine generated works, so that authors, readers, and others can easily identify trusted content and enjoy a transparent exchange of value for content.

1. US Copyright Office. *The Compendium of U.S. Copyright Office Practices: Chapter 300.* https://copyright.gov/comp3/chap300/ch300-copyrightable-authorship.pdf

RIGHT 8: THE RIGHT TO COPYRIGHT EDUCATION

Knowledge of copyright, its value and how to exploit and protect it is vital for every citizen, particularly in a digital age when we all are creators. We believe governments and relevant industry bodies have a role to play in spreading knowledge, understanding, and critical thinking skills around copyright issues.

Authors need education in publishing rights management, in creative enterprise and innovation including business and negotiation skills, and contract law as it pertains to copyright.

Also key is an understanding of the benefits of open access; Creative Commons licenses; the symbiotic nature of the creator-user relationship; the implications of author economic and moral rights in relation to trade-publishers, self-publishing services, and publishing contract law.

Those working in literary organizations need to understand the changed ecosystem for authors and the reality of how books are traded and read in the digital age. Many remain closed to independent authors, and it is time indie authors were included in their programs.

Readers need education in how to properly attribute and use copyright works and also in the value of copyright to writers and artists, in how to access works from genuine sources, and in the power of direct purchasing from the author by introduction (See ALLi's SelfPub3 Campaign, which encourages readers to buy ebooks directly from authors' websites at Allianceindependentauthors.org/selfpub3. See also Get it Right from a Genuine Site.

Article Eight: *Critical thinking and skills around copyright law, policy, and practice should be taught in every school, university, and community and particularly in literary and creative organizations and industries.*

THE FUTURE

The Alliance of Independent Author's *Copyright Bill of Rights* paints the possibility of a global copyright environment that balances the benefits of ownership with the flexibility to run a successful and sustainable online author business.

Many of the rights now enshrined in copyright law were hard won by author activists of the past. It is thanks to them that writers have been able to find dignity and livelihood within publishing, as the laws were modified and improved throughout the nineteenth, twentieth, and twenty-first centuries.

Today, as jurisdictions around the world work to update their copyright laws to keep pace with digital disruption, creative entrepreneurship, and the knowledge economy, we are at an important juncture for copyright policy and practice.

As *intellectual property law* has developed, it has generated much *contract law* and also, these days, much *electronic commerce law*. Copyright has expanded its power and reach, moved beyond the intent of its original conception, and seen a huge copyright clearance industry grow up around it.

Copyright once spurred novelty, creativity, and growth in our store of knowledge; now it restricts what can be made available in online libraries.

Once concerned with making it possible for authors to reach the widest possible readership, it now makes outlaws of millions of readers who post fan-fiction, or download or share free books.

Once an attempt to free authors from exploitation by printers and booksellers, and servile dependency on the patronage of church, state or royalty, it now tries to hand control back to Big Content publishers.

A myriad of social, technological, economic, and legal developments now see the copyright industry increasingly in conflict with critics, scholars, free expression activists, and the writers and artists it pertains to protect.

If legislators focus more on authors' rights, without an understanding of an author's relationship with their readers, or a realistic assessment of the modern business of books and their associated products, or how most entrepreneurial creators work, trade, and negotiate, they harm more than help authors and readers.

The law can mean one thing for an advantaged group and something quite different for those on society's margins or those disempowered by lack of knowledge, or trying to negotiate in conditions of unequal bargaining abilities or weight.

Just because authors own the rights doesn't mean they know how, or have the confidence, to exploit them. Just because anyone *can* self-publish now doesn't mean anyone *does* self-publish now.

Increased author confidence among self-publishing authors is now showing in the variety of business models they are adopting (see Appendix III), and the variety of content (not just text but audio and video) that many now publish on their websites.

Understanding this changed landscape is challenging for authors and the government bodies that support them: ministries responsible for business, entrepreneurship, culture, intellectual property, the knowledge economy, and related industry organizations. For example:

- Copyright legislators, governments, and most literary bodies think territorially, within legislative jurisdictions, but independent authors think globally. Independent authors

Copyright Bill of Rights

who live, write, publish, and claim copyright in one territory are selling to and interacting with readers and potential readers worldwide.
- Author-publishers may choose to offer their work freely and consider themselves to be working in "the gift economy," employing free sharing for ideological reasons, or so-called freemium models that ultimately generate a profit. Some even welcome piracy as a marketing strategy.
- Digital Rights Management (DRM) technology is useless in practice and most independent authors choose not to employ it, considering it an infringement on reader rights and an unnecessary inconvenience for their readers.

Moving copyright more firmly into the author's domain today relies on authors' ability to assert copyright, when signing contracts with publishing or self-publishing services, when negotiating with rights buyers, and when dealing with plagiarism and piracy.

Authors are not just creators and publishers. We are also content consumers, scholars, and citizens who acknowledge that public policy must consider and address these competing interests and ensure the preservation of a fair use/dealing environment, as well as free speech, on the internet.

New technologies like machine learning, translation and other AI, the blockchains and other tools are fast coming on track, with the power to shift economies, businesses and behaviors, and how authors trade, all over again.

More than ever, authors' advancement depends on their ability to think critically about how copyright supports their work in the digital age, as author business models evolve.

Anything that can be expressed as bits will be. I believe that bits exist to be copied. Therefore, I believe that any business model that depends on your bits not being copied is just dumb, and that lawmakers who try to prop these up are like governments that sink fortunes into protecting people who insist on living on the sides of active volcanoes.

ALLIANCE OF INDEPENDENT AUTHORS

— CORY DOCTOROW, CRAPHOUND.COM

Understanding this fast-changing landscape is challenging. But to be effective, contemporary copyright policy must be framed around how author-publishers actually work, trade, and negotiate today, and how today's readers actually discover, buy, and read books.

We must all get better at identifying, tracking, quantifying, and supporting independent authors as creative digital micro-businesses. This includes considering the impact on the independent author when reviewing and updating policy and legislation around issues such as copyright.

We seek the optimization of the value of the authors' moral and monetary rights not just through the assertion of copyright in intellectual property law, but its enforcement through contract and commercial law.

We urge interested parties from all sides—including authors—to better understand the trading environment and copyright challenges of the self-publishing author in a digital environment and how copyright policy, and its implementation, directly affects their ability to earn a living and contribute to the fabric of society.

We must guard against copyright becoming our contemporary equivalent of the medieval guild of printers and booksellers we'll introduce you to in Appendix I: "A Short History of Copyright". We need not just balance robust and flexible copyright law but also the education to understand what's at stake, and the means to interpret and assert the needs of authors, readers, scholars, and citizens.

We hope our *Copyright: Bill of Rights* will help further the debate and foster the critical thinking that will facilitate this end.

To read a list of resources which were most useful when establishing ALLi's position on copyright and compiling its bill of rights, please see Selfpublishingadvice.org/copyright-resources/

Copyright Bill of Rights

APPENDIX I: A SHORT HISTORY OF COPYRIGHT

The earliest documentary evidence of a contract between a 'publisher' and 'author' was in 1667 between John Milton and stationer Samuel Simmons for *Paradise Lost*[1]. The contract provided that Simmons was to pay Milton £5 on signing, another £5 when the first edition sold 1300 copies, £5 when the second edition sold 1300 copies, and a final £5 payment when the third edition sold 1300 copies. In exchange, Milton signed over to Simmons, *"All that Booke, Copy, or Manuscript"* of the poem, together with *"the full benefit, profit, and advantage thereof, or w[hic]h shall or may arise thereby."*

Milton had been a longtime critic of how printing was regulated in England. Stationers like Simmons were members of the Stationers' Guild, and included text writers, illustrators, bookbinders, and booksellers, which sold manuscripts or copies they had produced. The Stationers' Charter, which essentially enshrined a monopoly on book production, extended privilege to the printers of a book by ensuring no one else was entitled to "copy" a text once a member had asserted ownership.

In November, 1644, Milton had written *Areopagitica*, a protest against how printing was regulated in England by the Guild and to argue against a proposal in Parliament that would require licenses to print books. A pamphlet in the form of a speech supposed to be addressed to the Parliament, pointed out how the Guild's monopoly exploited writers and led to suppression and censorship which cheated readers of a diversity of expression.

John Milton died before he had received all the payments under his contract with Simmons. There is evidence of a small sum being paid to Milton's widow, and much ado about the state of poverty in which Milton's granddaughter was later forced to live. This debate contributed the world's first author-friendly copyright law.

The British Statute of Anne Copyright Act (1710)[2], the first fully-fledged copyright statute, granted "copyright" to the author of a book. This law was the result of a carefully considered balance of author's rights and public interests.

The intent of the new law of 1710 was to free authors from the dominance of the printers and booksellers and also from external support and patronage. This was for the sake of writers, yes, but also of readers.

The Statue of Anne was "An Act for the Encouragement of Learning". Its intent was that society would benefit from ideas, insights, and imaginative works being spread as widely as possible and that vesting upon authors and their assigns the "sole liberty of printing and reprinting their books," for a limited term was the best way to achieve this.

This considered statute of law, with its balance between authors' and purchasers' rights, has stood the test of time, influencing copyright legislation in several other nations, including the US, and is still frequently invoked by judges and academics today.

It originally prescribed a copyright term of fourteen years, with a provision for a one-time renewal for a second fourteen years, during which only the author and the printers to whom they chose to license their works could publish. After that maximum term of twenty-eight years, copyright would expire and the work fell into the public domain.

Later acts revised and consolidated this original legislation: lengthened the term of copyright to the author's life plus fifty (later seventy) years; extended its domain to other works including drama, music, engravings, paintings, drawings and, as technology expanded, photographs, sound recordings and film; expanded its remit throughout the Empire; and affirmed that copyright arose in the act of creation, not the act of publishing

The next most notable legal development was the Berne Convention for the Protection of Literary and Artistic Works, which attempted to coordinate copyright at the international level. It was heavily influenced by the French concept of *droit d'auteur*, and centered on authors rights, in contrast to the Anglo-American concept of copyright centering on economic concerns.

These two came together when American content creators, seeing the advantages in the European approach, decided in 1989, after a century of resistance, to become party to the Berne Convention.

Thus copyright law at the dawn of the digital revolution was moulded by two different traditions: a European creator-rights model, in which the intention was to assure authors' and rights holders' claims, much like the law protects physical property rights; and an Anglo-American consumer-rights tradition in which copyright is primarily concerned with what the Statue of Anne called the "Encouragement of Learning": giving readers and scholars easy access to a shared culture.

---

1. Deazley, R. (2008) 'Commentary on Milton's Contract 1667', in *Primary Sources on Copyright (1450-1900)*, eds L. Bently & M. Kretschmer, www.copyrighthistory.org
2. Wikipedia. https://en.wikipedia.org/wiki/Statute_of_Anne Accessed May 11, 2019

APPENDIX II: COPYRIGHT FAQS

Who Owns a Copyright?

As soon as you put original work down in writing, be it a shopping list, a funny limerick, or a bestselling novel, and whether on a pad of paper, a hard drive, a smartphone, or a recording device, you own the copyright for that creation. Your first draft, riddled with typos, inconsistencies, and clichés, is protected by copyright law whether or not you polish it, publish it, register it, or mark it with a ©. Original does not mean your work must be a unique masterpiece; it means you did not copy the expression of the work.

What Does Copyright Ownership Mean?

If anyone violates the exclusive rights described above, the copyright owner may have a claim of infringement. Of course, there are exceptions. There are always exceptions, and exceptions to the exceptions. The most common is fair use or fair dealing.

What Is Protected by Copyright Law?

Literary works; musical works including lyrics; dramatic works; pictorial, graphic, and sculptural works; sound recordings; architectural works; and pantomimes and choreographic works if fixed in tangible form such as a video recording.

What about characters and settings? Maybe. If a character is as fully developed as Harry Potter or a setting as distinctive as Panem in *The Hunger Games*, the creator might claim copyright protection.

What Is NOT Protected by Copyright Law?

It varies from country to country. In the Anglo-American world, titles, names, and short phrases are copyright free. So, sorry to say, your book's title is not protected by copyright in the US—that's why there are so many books with similar names. But when you publish in Germany, for example, your title is protected by copyright.

If you have a series with a distinctive name, like the *For Dummies* series, or a very famous title like *The Da Vinci Code*, you may have a trademark interest in the title, but only because that title has become associated in the minds of buyers with a particular book, or product, from a particular maker. Unlike copyright, trademark is not automatic. It gets its value by being used and known in the marketplace.

Objective information such as historical facts, test results, and statistics are not copyrightable, although the method of organization and analysis are. If you are writing non-fiction or historical fiction, real world facts and events are not protected. Anyone else may write about those same events, even if you were the one to discover them first.

Works not fixed into a tangible form of expression, such as improvisational performances and choreographic works that have not been written down or recorded, are copyright free. As are ideas, themes, and concepts, such as a spicy romance between a space alien and a movie star. This drives some writers crazy because they are sure their idea is worth millions and someone will steal it. But think about it. How many times have you had what feels like a million-dollar idea, but after writing ten pages or two pages, the idea peters out? What copyright protects is the execution and expression of the idea into a story, drama, movie, painting, or piece of music. Not the idea itself.

Stock characters and stereotypes, such as the tough-talking gangster or the handsome-but-dull hero, are not protected, because they are not considered original. Same with generic settings such as deep space or undersea worlds.

Must You Mark Your Work with ©?

Not technically, but do it anyway to put the world on notice of your ownership of the work. The copyright notice has three parts:

1. © or copyright.
2. Year of first publication, which means the year the work was first distributed to the public. On unpublished material, the notice reads "Unpublished Work © [year] [author]."
3. Name of copyright owner, which may be a pen name or the name of an entity such as a corporation. If there is more than one copyright owner, name all of them.

Also add "All Rights Reserved", because the phrase is required in some foreign countries. In Europe another common phrase is "The moral rights of the author have been asserted."

How Long Will Your Copyright Last?

In most countries a copyright lasts for the life of the author, plus fifty to seventy years. If there are two or more authors, use the life of the last surviving author, plus seventy years. The copyright passes to the heirs of the owners, just like any other property interest.

Many other highly developed countries, such as Japan, still have shorter terms.

Are Copyrights Transferrable?

Oh yes. And they are sliced and diced into various pieces. This happens most often in one of two ways:

- Assignment: when you transfer some or all of your rights to another party, for part or all of the copyright term.

- License: you retain ownership and maintain your rights but you give another party permission to use your work under certain conditions.[1]

An an indie author, we encourage you to learn how to navigate licensing and assignment of your rights in a way that both protects and benefits you.

Should You Register Your Work with Your Country's Copyright Office?

Registration is no longer mandatory in the US, has never been mandatory in Canada, and is not mandatory in any of the Berne Convention signatory countries. You will own the copyright in your work whether or not you register it. However, registration establishes a public, searchable record of your claim and is required in some countries before an infringement suit may be filed. In the US, prompt registration (within three months following publication) increases the potential damages recoverable in an infringement action.

Will Your Self-Publishing Service Company Own Your Copyright?

Not unless it is unscrupulous. When you engage an SPSC (self-publishing service company), or a direct distributor, you will not be (should not be) transferring any rights to it, other than the non-exclusive right to use your work to produce and distribute books for you, which may include the right to display and market it on its websites.

Should You Pay Your SPSC a Fee to Register Your Copyright for You?

No. And if a company is charging for this service, you should probably look elsewhere. There may well be other unnecessary add-ons in your package. See ALLi's guidebook *Choosing the Best Self-Publishing Companies and Services* at Selfpublishingadvice.org/choosebestservices/ for more on this, and John Doppler's blog post "12 Self-Publishing Services Authors Should Beware" at Selfpublishingadvice.org/services-beware/.

Fair Use/Dealing

Although copyright law gives you a great deal of control over who may use your work and how, you cannot prohibit all uses. People may use portions of your work for education, commentary, and even criticism, no matter how scathing. You may have to tolerate parody, even if it is offensive and distasteful.

The doctrines of fair use in the US and fair dealing in the UK protect these forms of speech, even when they incorporate your copyrighted work.

Fair dealing and fair use are defined as any copying of copyrighted material (even verbatim) for a limited purpose, such as commentary, criticism, education, or parody. Such uses may be done without permission from the copyright owner.

The concept of "fair dealing" was spelled out in the UK in the 1956 Copyright Act and reinforced in the 1988 Act, specifying that copyright work could be quoted, permission free, for the purpose of research, private study, reporting of current events, or for the purposes of criticism or review. In the US, fair use is considered a form of free speech protected by the First Amendment.

The line between fair use/dealing and infringement is murky. Much depends on the facts of the case, the aggressiveness of the copyright owner, and the temperament of the judge. There is no specific number of words that may be used without permission.

Non-commercial or educational use is not 100 percent safe, particularly if you use a substantial part of the original material.

Giving credit to the author does not make a difference—you could be infringing even if you are not plagiarizing.

In the US, courts take four factors into consideration. No one factor controls; they are weighed against one another.

1. **The purpose and character of the use.** Is the use commercial or for non-profit or educational purposes? Does the new work offer something above and beyond the original? The buzz word is *transformative*.
2. **The nature of the copyrighted work.** Is the original work factual or artistic? Reusing factual content is more likely to be fair use, while reusing artistic elements is not. Using unpublished works is less likely to be fair use due to the potential negative effect on the value of the original work.
3. **The amount and substantiality of the portion used in relation to the copyrighted work as a whole.** The more you use, the less likely it will be considered fair use, especially if you use the "heart" or "essence" of a work.
4. **The effect** of the use upon the potential market for, or value of, the copyrighted work.

Keep in mind that fair use applies only to copyrighted work. The portions of any work that are not subject to copyright—titles, objective information such as historical facts, data and test results, ideas and concepts—may be used regardless of fair use.

Here are some examples of uses that were NOT considered fair use.

- A book of trivia questions based upon the Seinfeld show.
- A Harry Potter encyclopedia.
- A news program showing one minute and fifteen seconds of the Rodney King beating. (In contrast, uses of still images

and clips of Abraham Zapruder's film of JFK's assassination have been considered fair use.)
- A parody of the OJ Simpson trial based on *The Cat in the Hat* by Dr. Seuss, because it used the book to parody a related event. In other words, the court ruled the writer could use *The Cat in the Hat* to make fun of the book itself, but not for making fun of something else.
- In contrast, 2 Live Crew's rap-style rewrite of Roy Orbison's "Oh, Pretty Woman" was considered a parody and fair use because it poked fun at the song itself.[2]

As you can see, the cases are not entirely consistent. The safest course is to get permission from the copyright owner. Even if you are well within safe lines, the copyright owner might sue you anyway. Fair use is a defence. If you are sued, you will have the burden of proving fair use. Think of the attorney's fees and the time involved. While we admire those who take on David and Goliath fights, we'd rather spend our time writing our next books.

---

1. Canadian Intellectual Property Office, https://www.ic.gc.ca/eic/site/cipointernet-internetopic.nsf/eng/wr00054.html Accessed May 12, 2019
2. 2 Live Crew. *Pretty Woman parody.* http://www.youtube.com/watch?v=65GQ70Rf_8Y

APPENDIX III: BUSINESS MODELS FOR AUTHORS
APPENDIX

As technology expands, it creates more opportunities for authors to make a living in a variety of ways from their writing—no matter what kind of books they write, or what kind of publisher they are. At ALLi, we call this transition of authors from professionals to author-businesses SelfPub3.

Copyright law has made it possible for authors to earn from their books, and it is the foundation on which each of these business models rest.

Here are some of the most common business models employed by successful indie authors today.

1. Books Only, One Outlet: Write Fast, Publish Often

Writing in a popular genre, writing fast, publishing often. For many genre fiction authors, this model of writing fast and publishing often has become mainstream in the last few years.

It is not new. The 19th and 20th century "sensation stories" for weekly tabloids that Louisa May Alcott criticized in *Little Women* and "pulp publishers" who produced massive amounts of escapist fiction on cheap 'pulp' paper so the price could be kept low, drew on writers who could work in this way.

Today they work for themselves, often publishing through Amazon to take advantage of KU (Kindle Unlimited) and other exclusive benefits.

2. Books Only, Going Wide: Multiple Formats and Retailers

Referred to in the community as "going wide", this is publishing through Kobo, Apple Books, Google Play, and/or aggregator distributors like Draft2Digital and PublishDrive as well as KDP for ebooks. And using IngramSpark and KDP Print for print books.

Authors operating this model also publish in multiple formats: ebook, print, audio. The idea is to reach as many readers as possible by being available in all retailers, all possible geographies, and all formats, and to build a growing readership, steadily, over time.

Income Streams

Authors can supplement their book income by adding other income streams to these business models. These income streams typically are (but not limited to):

- Freelancing - Writing, copywriting etc.
- Journalism - print, podcasting/radio, video/TV
- Publishing Services - Editing, formatting, design etc.
- Referrals/affiliate marketing
- Speaking and appearances
- Sponsorship or other influencer income
- Teaching writing or publishing craft

3. The Creator Model

The creator economy sees authors taking charge of their platform. This includes selling directly to readers, and incorporating various products and services alongside their books e.g. premium digital content (including NFTs on a choice of blockchains), subscriptions, memberships, reader clubs, paid video and audio content, as well as crowdfunders and patronage. As of 2023, 12.6% indies use this model. This is the fastest growing sector not just in publishing but also throughout the creative industries.

The advantage of this model is dependable income from many readers and fans. You can mould your publishing business around your interests and talents, and the needs of your readers. The downside is that reader expectations need to be managed so that they don't interfere with your creative process.

4. Rights Licensing Model

In this model, in addition to publishing your own books, you license your publishing rights to third-party rights buyers. This model works for authors who have established author platforms already. But if you limit the format, term, and territory, you can license a variety of rights, across the world, to maximize your income.

The advantage of this model is that your licensing partners bring expertise and new opportunities which expand the reach of your book. The disadvantage is the need to be constantly pitching and vigilant about all contracts and agreements. 6.6% of indies are using this strategy in their business in 2023.

5. Publisher Model

Authors employing this model not only publish their own books but other authors too, becoming a third-party publisher themselves, on a traditional publishing (licensing authors' rights and paying royalties) or hybrid publishing (charging for publishing services) model. 2.4% of authors employ this business model in 2023. This business model is highly reliant on your personal mission and values.

The upside of this is the ability to trade in more work that you can ever produce yourself, making your publishing business more sustainable and stable. The downside is the management and responsibility of other writers' careers.

You can mix these business models to create one that fits you uniquely. Remember, your books are just a starting point. And you can create experiences your readers will love.

To learn more about these publishing business models and author businesses, see ALLi's Author Business campaign guide, **SelfPub3**. This guide is available to download in the Members' Zone for free, or could be purchased at Selfpublishingadvice.org/books/selfpub3/

APPENDIX IV: COPYRIGHT ORGANIZATIONS & TREATIES

Organizations

WIPO World Intellectual Property Organization

UNESCO United Nations Educations, Scientific & Cultural Organization

WTO World Trade Organization

EU European Union

IFRRO International Federation of Reproduction Rights Organisations

IPA International Publishers Association

AIPLA American Intellectual Property Law Association

ALAI Association Litteraire et Artistique Internationale

CISAC International Confederation of Societies of Authors and Composers

Foundational Copyright Treaties

The Berne Convention: copyright treaty originating 1886, revised in 1908, 1928, 1948, 1967, 1971, and 1979.

WIPO Copyright Treaty (WCT): addresses distribution of digital works over the internet, and two issues not addressed by Berne: computer programs and data compilations. Requires member countries to guard against removal of rights management measures incorporated into technology.

WIPO Performance and Phonograms Treaty (WPPT): addresses the rights of performers and producers in the digital space.

Newer Copyright Treaties

Beijing Treaty on Audiovisual Performances: regulates audiovisual performances, will not enter into force until ratified by at least thirty member countries.

Marrakesh Treaty to Facilitate Access to Published Works for Persons Who Are Blind, Visually Impaired, or Otherwise Print Disabled : deals with copyright limitations and exceptions, rather than rights for creators.

Universal Copyright Convention (non-WIPO): drafted in 1952, a less-demanding convention than Berne, for those countries whose domestic copyright legislation does not meet the minimum requirements of Berne. Under UCC, copyright protection is not automatic in all UCC countries upon protection in the author's own country. The UCC requirement that all works produced with the authority of the author carry the © symbol, name of the copyright owner, and the year of first publication, is the origin of the practice of applying the copyright symbol.

To read a list of resources which were most useful when establishing ALLi's position on copyright and compiling its bill of rights, please see Selfpublishingadvice.org/copyright-resources/

ACKNOWLEDGMENTS

All good books are a team effort. An author's name goes on the cover but behind that is the creative team of editors and designers and formatters who made the book, the distributors and marketers who take it to readers, and the long list of supporters—from family members to work colleagues—without whom it would never have been created.

Then there are the other writers, from journalists and academics to storytellers and poets, who have published relevant ideas, information and inspirations that, quite literally, underwrite the book.

All this is true for this book you hold in your hand, and our thanks to all those who had a hand in its making.

For this campaign guide, particular thanks to the creative team: editor Bonnie Wagner Stafford, designer Jane Dixon-Smith, publishing assistant Sarah Begley, and proofreader Shanaya Wagh. Our small team used little support of ChatGPT, to make sure we had thought through all the facets of copyright.

And finally to all at the Alliance of Independent Authors (ALLi). ALLi guides rely heavily on the work and wisdom of our members, ambassadors, and advisors. The advice in our guides has often been published first on our blog, which they write, and draws also on their discussions in ALLi member forums, and on interviews with them about their writing and publishing experiences.

All of this is generously and freely shared with our non-profit CIC (Community Interest Company) with the intention of paying it forward, and benefitting other indie authors.

To them, and to all at ALLi: thank you for your generosity and for lighting the way.

If you found this guide useful, please give it a quick review on your preferred retailer.

We really appreciate your feedback. It helps us create better guidebooks for the indie community and helps other authors know that the book is worth their time.

For more resources on copyright and the legal cases mentioned in this book, please see SelfPublishingAdvice.org/copyright-resources

OTHER GUIDES

Browse and buy more publishing guides for indie authors on our website: SelfPublishingAdvice.org/Bookshop

ABOUT ALLI

The Alliance of Independent Authors (ALLi) is the only global, non-profit association for self-publishing writers. ALLi aims to foster excellence and ethics in self-publishing; to support authors in the making and selling of their books; and to advocate for author independence through the building of sustainable digital businesses.

ALLi is pronounced "ally" (al-eye not al-ee), and we aim to be an ally to self-publishers everywhere. We unite thousands of beginner, emerging, and experienced indie authors from all over the world behind this mission. Most of our members are in the US and Canada, followed closely by Europe, Australia and New Zealand, and South Africa. We are a Community Interest Company (CIC) and all profits are invested back in for the benefit of our members and the wider indie author community.

Our work is fourfold:

- ALLi *advises*, providing best-practice information and education through our online Self-Publishing Advice Center, SelfPublishingAdvice.org, offering a daily blog, a weekly live video and podcast, a bookstore of self-publishing guidebooks, and a quarterly member magazine.
- ALLi *monitors* the self-publishing sector through a watchdog desk, alerting authors to bad actors and predatory players and running an approved partner program.
- ALLi *campaigns* for the advancement of indie authors in the publishing and literary sectors globally (bookstores, libraries, literary events, prizes, grants, awards, and other author organizations), encouraging the provision of

publishing and business skills for authors, speaking out against iniquities and inequities, and furthering the indie author cause wherever possible.
- ALLi *empowers* independent authors through community and collaboration—author forums, contract advice, sample agreements, contacts and networking, literary agency representation, and a member care desk.

Learn more about the Alliance of Independent Authors on our member website found at Allianceindependentauthors.org and the Self-Publishing Advice Center which is available for all indie authors at Selfpublishingadvice.org/about.

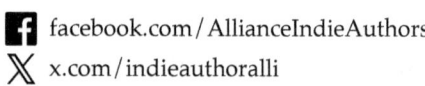

facebook.com/AllianceIndieAuthors
x.com/indieauthoralli

www.ingramcontent.com/pod-product-compliance
Lightning Source LLC
Chambersburg PA
CBHW071316080526
44587CB00018B/3246